FULL BLOOM

7 Practical Steps to Get What You Want

+ 1 to Grow On

NINA DURFEE

[inside front cover - blank]

FULL BLOOM

*7 Practical Steps
to Get What You Want*

$+$ 1 to Grow On

NINA DURFEE

Duvall, Washington 98019

First Edition Published 2011

ISBN XXX-XXXXXXXX

Cover art adapted from original e-book cover design by Imagine! Studios, LLC, www.artsimagine.com. Interior book design by Visual Communication, www.vizcomdesign.com.

Author photos courtesy of Simply Stated Photography by Joni Atkinson, www.simplystatedphotograph.com.

Dedication

This book is for women who have put their desires and passions on hold to raise families, tend to careers, manage households, and volunteer for worthy and not-so-worthy causes.

You know who you are. Your nest is emptying and your hormones are in disarray. The ideals you so clearly aspired to in your youth seem elusive at best. You ask, "What is my purpose? Is this as good as it gets? When will it be my turn? What do I want to be when I grow up?" Something deep inside you aches to be identified, enlivened, nurtured and expressed. You fear the very change you crave. You feel as if you've lived life by default, and you wonder if it's too late for anything else.

I dedicate this book to women of every age who seek to **live not by default, but by design**!

In Appreciation

I deeply appreciate the roles of the following people in my quest for spiritual satisfaction:

Cousin Patty, who taught me that when two people think differently neither is right or wrong. They are only different, and different is okay.

Kristiina Hiukka, who helped me find a spark of hope to fan into flames of enthusiasm.

Judge Mary Mertens James, who recognized my spark and encouraged me to fan it.

Anna, Diane and Melanie, who appreciate me, who hold my feet to the fire, and who continue to inspire me.

Esther and Jerry Hicks, who playfully drag me kicking and screaming into what they call the "Vortex of creation."

My father, who was the springboard from which I launched so many desires.

My mother, for her eternal softness and wisdom and whom I want to be just like when I grow up.

Myriad Universal forces that assembled to make my dreams reality.

My husband, David, for loving me no matter what, who all along has embodied all that I have tried so long to convince him is true. Turns out I was the one who needed convincing!

Table of Contents

Full Bloom – by Nina Durfee

Forward

The purpose of this book is to share my discovery of a process to get what you want. *Discovery* stems from the Latin word *discooperire*, "to uncover or disclose" something that is already there. Not one of these seven-plus-one steps is new. They have always existed. I simply set them out here to spark your attention so that you can put them to work in your favor.

As my boys began leaving for college, I anticipated an "empty nest." I was desperate to make a change but thought I was out of options. I was sleep deprived from hot flashes that barreled over me hourly like a runaway train. I felt trapped in a job I detested, surrounded by grumpy co-workers and mentally drained in a profession that no longer interested me. Even though my husband and I were both employed full time, our income barely met expenses, and our credit card balance was on an upward spiral. I didn't want a new job — I wanted a new way of living! I knew there was more to life, but I didn't know what it was or how to find it. I was ready to run screaming into the street!

A compassionate soul introduced me to a life coach whom I sat with at a table in Starbucks and blubbered for an hour, feeling as if I were encased in a concrete vault. At the end of our meeting I could detect a tiny pinprick of light through the concrete barrier. I knew something was on the other side, but I didn't know what. I didn't know how to reach it, but with my coach's skillful prompts and inquiries I felt the tickle of possibility.

I embarked on a fascinating journey of self-discovery. In addition to working with a coach, I did all the exercises in dozens of self-help books. I attended workshops in person and by telephone. With the gracious support of my loving husband I racked up thousands of dollars more credit card debt to complete my training as a life coach. I crafted vision

boards and repeated positive affirmations. I tacked sticky notes to the steering wheel and listened to inspirational CDs. I filled dozens of spiral binders with introspective journaling. In *The Last Lecture*, Randy Pausch tells us the brick walls are not there to trap us. Rather, he says, "The brick walls are there to show us how badly we want something." I made a list of the things I wanted:

- A bigger house (ours was only 700 square feet!)
- Big water views
- Lifework that feels meaningful and satisfying
- Trustworthy vehicles
- Financial comfort
- Move to the Puget Sound area
- Closer proximity to loved ones
- Mental clarity
- To feel understood
- Physical energy and good health
- To be a published writer
- Less stress
- More ease and flow
- NO MORE HOT FLASHES!

Within two years I looked back and realized that *every bit of my wish list* had come to be — not just the material things, but a deeply satisfying enrichment of spirit as well. People who knew me before and after this span of time scratched their heads in amazement. "That's incredible!" they said. "How did you do it?"

At first blush the answer is that I tried really, really hard. I'd been raised with the American work ethic: "the early bird gets the worm," "life is a struggle," "getting ahead is hard work." It made sense to believe that the only way any individual's dreams come true is through blood, sweat and tears, or as Malcolm Gladwell says in his award-winning book, *Outliers*, "through 10,000 hours of practice." And though I was in awe of how many of my dreams had "manifested" in just two years, my process had been a chaotic combination of turbulent trial and error. In the 20/20 clarity of hindsight I have sifted out the gems that brought me the most

Full Bloom – by Nina Durfee

mileage. If I had known these seven-plus-one steps before I began my journey, I'd have achieved all this much sooner and with greater ease. Knowing what I know now, through my own experience, makes the continuing journey less turbulent, more satisfying and just plain fun!

It happens that my steps include the three-step process described by Esther and Jerry Hicks (translators of the Teachings of Abraham) as the "Law of Attraction": (1) Ask; (2) It is given; (3) Allow. I know now that this simple 1-2-3 process is complete unto itself. Still, the do-er in me itches to get my hands in the clay, to feel as if I'm earning my end result. As a do-er I wondered how on earth do I simply allow?

Through much determination and effort (or perhaps in spite of it) things began working out for me in tangible ways. In retrospect I have tracked this process and am eager to share my learning with you. I have pinpointed a few practical steps that I consistently applied, actions that helped me anchor the basics and feel a sense (however misguided) of "control" in the process.

I attribute my success to the application of these steps, and it is my delight to set them out here for your use and enjoyment. This seven-plus-one-step process offers structure and orderliness. It makes me feel in charge and capable. If you follow these steps, you will get results. I guarantee it!

— Nina —

Introduction

Into the Garden

*Life finds its purpose and fulfillment
in the expansion of happiness.*
Maharishi Mahesh Yogi

Life is a garden. We are the gardeners who plan, create and reap the life of plenty that feeds our physical, mental, emotional and spiritual hunger.

We have the power to choose what we want, the tools to prepare our creative soil, to plant the seed of ideas and dreams and to sprinkle the water that clarifies our intention. Our powers of observation and recognition are the sunshine and fertilizer that nurture our desire to maturity. Plentiful harvest rewards our deliberate action and offers a parting gift: seeds to create more, perpetuating the plenty.

When all is said and done — it is never done! There is always more to want, a higher plateau to reach, a greater thrill to seek. As wonderful as each end result is, the greatest joy is in the process of tending our garden, feeling the whoosh of the miraculous cycle of life and the bliss of catching up with a dream, only to launch another.

*Happiness is the meaning and the purpose of life,
the whole aim and end of human existence.*
Aristotle

Full Bloom - by Nina Durfee

STEP 1
Be Still – Tilling the Soil

All creative endeavor is born from creative stillness.
Eckhart Tolle

Before we can have, we must do.
Before we can do, we must think.
Before we can think, we must **be**.

How many thoughts go through your head every hour? Before you picked up this book, your brain sent a signal to your hand. Before engaging, you contemplated at lightening speed a whole stream of "what's in it for me" thoughts. In addition, a variety of unrelated thoughts weaved through the tangle. "Is this the right time, what should I be doing instead, I'm thirsty, will this book finally solve my problems, I need to get the oil changed, I like the word *practical* in the title, I forgot to call Mom, I don't have time for this, what the heck, I'll just thumb through it."

Given the speed and quantity of thoughts present in nearly every moment, it's a wonder we accomplish anything at all!

Replace mental busyness with mental silence.

Before planting her crop, the gardener tills and aerates the soil to eliminate the rocks and weeds that inhibit fertile growth. Silence is the aerator that clears away mental busyness, worry, anticipation and fear. Silence creates mental breathing space.

Mental silence comes not by doing, but by not doing. When we let go of thought, we let go of resistance, and it feels good. Letting go of thought is not as easy as it sounds. Fortunately, there are a number of techniques designed to accomplish that very thing.

Take a bath of solitude on a daily basis.
Tanga Cleeve
www.onandoffthemat.com

Meditation feels good, and it is good for you.

A 2011 article entitled "Meditation: A Simple, Fast Way to Reduce Stress"[1] written by Mayo Clinic staff members claims: "Meditation is considered a type of mind-body complementary medicine. [It] produces a deep state of relaxation and a tranquil mind. During meditation, you focus your attention and eliminate the stream of jumbled thoughts that may be crowding your mind and causing stress. This process results in enhanced physical and emotional well-being."

When we meditate we let go of resistance. Releasing resistance feels like relief. Relief feels good. Meditation feels good!

Mayo Clinic staff members published another article entitled "Meditation: Take a Stress-Reduction Break Wherever You Are," in which they claim: "[S]ome research suggests that meditation may help such conditions as allergies, anxiety disorders, asthma, binge eating, cancer, depression . . . heart disease, high blood pressure, sleep problems and substance abuse."

Meditation's value is best measured by its effects on activity. Meditation releases stress, increases energy, improves physical health and helps us sleep better and think more clearly. Mental clarity increases productivity and effectiveness and makes for better communication, which improves personal and business relationships. Meditation increases overall wellbeing and peace of mind.

What kind of meditation is right for me?

Multiple methods exist and here are just a few:

- Japa meditation (employs a mantra)
- Dhayna or Samadhi meditation (concentration)
- "Brain Wave Vibration" (moving meditation)
- Prayer (contemplation)
- Vipassana meditation (insight/mindfulness)
- Zen meditation
- Yoga (movement)

---

[1] http://www.mayoclinic.com/health/meditation/HQ01070/NSECTIONGROUP=2

I practice Transcendental Meditation™ because it is easy and it feels good mentally and physically. There are also a variety of guided meditations, my favorite being the one offered by the Hickses in their book, *Getting into the Vortex: Guided Meditations CD and User Guide*. I say, find mental relaxation however you can — take a walk, say the Rosary, pet the dog, gaze at the stars.

Options abound. Do the research, experiment and choose your own adventure!

> *Silence is the mother of truth.*
> Benjamin Disraeli

Recap

Before we can have, we must do.
Before we can do, we must think.
Before we can think, we must be.

- Replace mental busyness with mental silence.
- Meditation feels good.
- Meditation has positive health benefits.
- Meditation techniques abound. Explore, experiment and choose what you enjoy.

TRY THIS

Enjoy Mental Stillness

- Eliminate disturbances for a few minutes — turn off the phone, hang a do-not-disturb sign on the door.

- Sit comfortably upright in a chair and close your eyes.

- Breathe in easily to a slow count of three, imagining clarity, rejuvenation, and wellbeing washing through you.

- Breathe out easily to a slow count of five, releasing worry, doubt and fear. Enjoy the feeling of relief.

- Continue for several minutes with your attention easily on your breath. Thoughts will come. When you are aware of them, simply shift your attention back to the breath.

- Slowly open your eyes.

- Appreciate how you feel in the moment. Notice the difference it makes in your day.

Repeat daily for 10-20 minutes.

STEP 2
Think – Planting the Seed

The indispensable first step to getting the things you want out of life is this: Decide what you want.
Ben Stein

Step 2 in the get-what-you-want process is: THINK.

But wait – didn't we just spend an entire chapter on how to stop thinking? Why, suddenly, is thought an important step? Let's reiterate the basic premise:

> Before we can have, we must do.
> Before we can do, we must **think.**
> Before we can think, we must be.

Thought determines outcome.

Tilled, fertile ground welcomes what comes its way: dandelion fluff blowing in on the breeze, an acorn dropped by a scurrying squirrel, a buried root determined to reemerge. The dandelion is beautiful in its own right, but if you want a sunflower you must deliberately plant a sunflower seed.

Thought is the seed that determines outcome. You get what you think about.

My own experience blatantly evidences the truth of this concept, so much so that I was delighted to stumble across references by multiple authors and mentors to the very law that governs the process: the Law of Attraction.

In their book *The Law of Attraction*, Esther and Jerry Hicks define the Law of Attraction as "that which is like unto itself is drawn." They explain that you get the essence of what you think about whether you want it or not. In my experience, elements that affect the power of attraction include:

Thought – intellectual activity in the form of consideration, reflection, contemplation, recollection

Expectation – not what you think should happen, but what you regard as likely

Feeling/emotion – internal perception by means other than sight, hearing, taste, smell or touch

Belief – certainty, conviction and acceptance as true (whether or not susceptible to rigorous proof)

Focus – your central point of attention or activity

Random thoughts produce random action and random results.

Are your thoughts pertinent to what you want next, or are they a jumble of unrelated ideas? Are they habitual? Are they your own or do they belong to your ancestors? Are you thinking by default or by design?

> *Whatever we put our attention on*
> *will grow stronger in our life.*
> Maharishi Mahesh Yogi

Action without clear, intentional thought yields less than satisfactory results. Leaping before looking offers a certain thrill, but the outcome of such random action is unpredictable, frequently undesirable and at times even catastrophic. Satisfying action demands deliberate thought.

Thoughts you keep thinking become your beliefs.

Webster defines *belief* as "an opinion or conviction." Hicks clarifies the definition: "A belief is just a thought you keep thinking."

Why are beliefs important? Beliefs mold our reality. People we trust (parents, teachers, religious traditions, etc.) imply something is true and the repetition of these ideas embeds them in our thinking. Soon we take our beliefs for granted and they become our truth. We establish a habit of thought and behavior based on our "truth," often unconsciously. We believe, and our beliefs steer our decisions and choices. Some beliefs serve us well. Others keep us stuck in a confining rut.

Full Bloom – by Nina Durfee

Whether you think you can or think you can't,
either way you are right.
Henry Ford

According to Shad Helmstetter, author of *What to Say When You Talk To Your Self*, "The more we believe about something, the more we will accept other ideas which are similar." Repeated specific thought about anything, including yourself, shores up its believability. Helmstetter says, "The longer you have bought the thought, the 'truer' it is."

What mental tapes do you play over and over?
Nothing ever works out for me.
I'm so clumsy.
I never remember names.
Whatever I eat goes straight to my thighs.
I can't afford it.
I don't have enough time.
Everyone's got the flu, I'm probably next.
Nobody cares what I think.
The older I get, the more things go wrong.
The longer I live, the less I can do.

In *Change Your Brain, Change Your Life*, Daniel G. Amen, M.D., tells us: "Thoughts have actual physical properties. They are real! They have significant influence on every cell in your body. When your mind is burdened with many negative thoughts, it affects your deep limbic system and causes deep limbic problems (irritability, moodiness, depression, etc.). Teaching yourself to control and direct thoughts in a positive way is one of the most effective ways to feel better."

What mental tapes do you want to hear instead?
Things have a way of working out for me.
I'm getting better at remembering names.
I enjoy eating what makes me feel good.
I feel abundant in many ways.
I don't have to do everything right now.
I enjoy staying healthy.
My opinion matters as much as the next guy's.
I like watching people who age gracefully.
Some people dance into their nineties!

The tilled field of the quiet mind is the perfect space to consciously plan, select and determine outcome. This is the place to choose not only that you want a garden, but that you specifically want tomatoes, Swiss chard, eggplant or sunflowers. This is the time to clarify not only that you want more money, but that you want the freedom of time and activity it allows. This is a chance to claim not only that you want a better career, but that you want to feel confident, exhilarated, creative and focused.

Thoughts become things. Choose the good ones.
Mike Dooley

The thoughts you think over and over become subliminal messages that inform and direct your action and your experience. Repeated thought ensures repeated outcome.

To change the outcome, change your thoughts.

Attention to what specifically is in the way, including fear, doubt, insecurity, lack of knowledge or limited resources, only amplifies the blockage. Create a new pattern of experience by engaging a new pattern of thought.

Recognize old thoughts and behaviors as they arise. Be willing to let go of what keeps you stuck. I'm not talking about putting up your dukes in active resistance to unwanted thought. Instead, simply turn your attention from what feels burdensome to what feels better, even exhilarating. Energize your thoughts and I promise you will enhance your outcome.

All we are is the result of what we have thought.
The Dhammapada (sayings of the Buddha)

Repetition ensures success.

A single positive thought may or may not produce the outcome you desire. But think it enough times and you reach what Malcolm Gladwell explores in his book by the same name, a "tipping point," a critical mass that changes the landscape. Craft a new pattern of thought, give it consistent attention until it becomes a belief, and it naturally becomes your new default. How cool is that!

What you think, you become.
Mohandas Gandhi

Recap

- Thought determines outcome.
- Random thoughts produce random action and random results.
- Thoughts you keep thinking become your beliefs.
- To change the outcome, change your thoughts.
- Repetition ensures success.

TRY THIS

Program Your Self-Talk

- For a week, keep a log of self-talk that emerges automatically in your thoughts or speech.

- For each negative self-talk statement, script a statement that feels both better and *possible*.

- Slip the restatement into your thought and speech daily.

- Notice what happens.

- Celebrate change!

STEP 3

Feel – Sprouting of the Seed

If it feels good, do it!
Woodstock Philosophy

Why do some seeds remain dormant while others pop open and emerge from the earth? How can you ensure your thoughts will sprout into productive actions?

Feeling inspires action.

*At the heart of every desire
is the desire to feel good.*
Esther and Jerry Hicks

Feeling is the energy that sprouts the seed of thought into action. Thought without feeling is objective and benign. The thought of sunflowers may include color, texture, size, shape or genetic strain. Those are inert clinical facts.

Feeling energizes the inert. Feeling is the spiritual spark detected as a tickle, a whisper, an itch, a belly flip that tells you *why* you want sunflowers. Maybe the color and shape delight you; or the tall stalks stir a childhood memory of awe at a flower "bigger than me;" or the flutter of birds among the blossoms feels lively and energizing; or the anticipation of savoring the roasted seeds evokes the ease of a lazy summer day in the ballpark bleachers. You want sunflowers because in so many ways they make you feel good.

Why adds incentive and momentum.

Awareness of *why* you want what you want releases resistance. Feel the subtle difference between wanting something because you don't have it and wanting something because of how you will feel when you do have it. The slight shift from negative to positive kicks universal forces into gear. People, circumstances and mysterious forces I cannot prove to a scientist gather together to energize the dream.

I had a client whose passion for artistic collage was squelched by the overwhelming energy drain due to an unfulfilling job, caring for an aging parent and frequent bouts of fibromyalgia. Her basement was filled with boxes of art supplies but she had no room to access them and put them to use. Her husband urged her to get rid of all of it since it was just taking up valuable space.

For my client, the thought of giving away (and giving up) her artistic dreams was as painful as the thought of giving away her own child. Yet the supplies lay dormant and inaccessible. She was locked in anguished paralysis, unable to take any action at all.

I asked her if time, space and money were no object, what would be her vision. She saw herself in a home studio, artistically organized and supplied, joyfully crafting unique cards, journals and charms with antique papers and trinkets. She felt the freedom and flow of creativity, the opening of her heart and the full richness of passionate life unfolding. As she described her dream, her eyes and complexion brightened, her voice lightened and physical tension visibly dissipated. But the thought of the monumental task of sorting the boxes brought her right back to a full stop.

I asked her to envision the studio of her dreams and to commit to open and sort one box — what to keep, what to sell, what to donate — with no obligation to ever open another box if she didn't want to.

That single act began a momentum that involved clearing out a room in her house and consciously equipping and decorating with enough supplies to begin some creative dabbling. Soon she was giving away beautiful handmade gifts and even selling some of her work on the internet.

She held the vision of the studio and why she wanted it — for the feeling of freedom and the flow of passionate creativity. She allowed the process to evolve rather than dutifully forcing it. She has since been relieved of the burden of draining full-time employment and is purchasing a new home with an enclosed patio that has plenty of natural light. The enclosed patio will become her art studio.

Full Bloom – by Nina Durfee

Adding *why* broadens the perspective from what you want to have into who you will be because of it. Use the **Feelings Menu** at the end of this chapter to help you articulate why you want what you want.

You can change how you feel.

Feelings are thrust upon us as a result of outside circumstances, right? Someone is rude to me, so I feel angry and disrespected. The college tuition is due, so I worry about making ends meet. I can't change how things make me feel, can I?

Yes, you can! And it is not a smoke-and-mirror parlor trick — but it's equally magical. Here are some ways to shift from feeling negative and helpless to feeling positive and powerful.

Remember

Memory is a powerful feeling inducer. It takes you right to the visceral place of experience.

My Dad was a flight instructor, and as a teenager I had the privilege of taking flight lessons. In one particularly memorable lesson in steep-banked turns — a delicate three-dimensional balance of roll (controlled by the ailerons), pitch (controlled by the elevators), and yaw (controlled by the rudder) — I turned the plane with wings tilted 60 degrees from horizontal. In doing so I allowed the nose to dip lower than the tail. In keeping with the laws of physics and aerodynamics, the plane proceeded to spin toward the earth. G-forces made me lightheaded, nauseous and disoriented. I couldn't tell up from down and I panicked. I vividly remember screaming and throwing up my hands in defeat. Then I blacked out. Needless to say, Dad righted the plane, I regained consciousness and I live to tell the story. (Thanks, Dad!) When I regained consciousness, my body and clothes were sopping wet. To this day that vivid memory makes me break out in a sweat.

Memory of a negative event induces negative feelings. You can use an uplifting memory to induce positive feelings. If you desire financial abundance, shift focus from lack ("I can't afford it") to abundance. What will abundance feel like for you? Luxurious? Exhilarating? Tap a memory that evokes those feelings, like the *exhilaration* of free-fall in a roller

coaster or the *luxury* of sleeping in on a cold winter morning. Choose whatever memories work for you. These memories won't fill your bank account, but they can line you up with the feeling of abundance.

Because like attracts like, an authentic feeling of abundance will draw abundance to you in many forms, including financial ease. The memory method works if you can tap memories that evoke genuine feelings of abundance. But what if you've never had an experience equivalent to what you want to evoke? What then? In the immortal word of John Lennon…

Imagine

When I was little and stubbed a toe or scraped an elbow, Dad would say, "Think how good that's gonna feel when it quits hurting!" It made me laugh every time. That simple shift from negative to positive changed my experience from pain to ease and from anguish to optimism. Imagination is a powerful feeling shifter.

> *Imagination is everything.*
> *It is the preview of life's coming attractions.*
> Albert Einstein

One of my coaching clients came to me feeling stuck in "procrastination mode." She needed to plan a vacation and couldn't bring herself to take the first step. She knew the time frame, knew the tropical destination and knew she wanted her daughter and grandson to accompany her. But she found the logistics, the phone calls to arrange flights, hotels, cars, lodging, what to pack, etc., were all too overwhelming. When I asked her what one thing she needed to know before beginning, she said, "I'm not sure what days my daughter can get away." As rational as it would have been to pick up the phone and call her daughter, my client remained stuck in a funk. In that familiar mindset she simply would not pick up the phone.

I asked her to close her eyes and imagine that all the details were already taken care of. I asked her to tell me about the vacation. She described the color of the ocean and the sand, lounging in a beach chair holding hands and enjoying a cocktail with her husband, watching their daughter and grandson play in the sun and surf. As she weaved this vision, her voice relaxed, her body relaxed, her tension dissipated. She released resistance.

Full Bloom – by Nina Durfee

Her buoyancy inspired her to pick up the phone, and the rest followed like falling dominoes. Moral of that story: when you want to shift to a better feeling, put yourself "on the beach"!

Affirmations: de-programming by re-programming

An affirmation, according to *Webster's Dictionary,* is "the assertion that something exists or is true." Recent convention defines affirmation as a present-tense statement designed to create a positive outcome or experience. Used this way, affirmations are effective tools to convert destructive thinking into productive thinking. But thought alone is not enough.

Guy Spiro, publisher of *The Monthly Aspectarian* and a proponent of the power of affirmations, says it is not thought alone that creates outcome. "Just as important as what we are thinking is *how we are feeling.*" Spiro goes on to say, "The emotional level is between the mental and the physical, touching both. I've often said that thinking positively while feeling negative is like putting frosting on a turd." A crude visual, to be sure, but it does speak to why affirmations in their initial stages may not feel true. Why? The element of expectation or belief is missing.

An affirmation that is too far removed from our current experience is difficult to swallow. But do not underestimate the power of the mind. I have found that we get what we believe and expect. Craft a general statement that feels possible rather than a specific statement that feels untrue. Soften "I'm a master gymnast" to "I'm getting better with practice."

> *A likely impossibility is always preferable*
> *to an unconvincing possibility.*
> Aristotle

How to Craft an Affirmation

First, decide what you want to change. For example, "I want to lose weight."

Describe how the change will make you feel. For example, I'll feel toned and flexible. My joints won't hurt. I'll have fewer sick days. I'll look good in my clothes.

Put those concepts into one or more first-person, present tense statements. For example, I move easily with energy and grace. I like how I look in the mirror. I feel light and healthy.

Assess the statement for what comedian Stephen Colbert has called "truthiness." If saying "I move easily with energy and grace" feels untrue, generalize it to make it more believable. "Moving gracefully is getting easier for me."

Physical Posturing

Wouldn't it be great if all you had to do to shift from sadness to happiness were to change your facial expression? Conclusions of studies conducted by Paul Ekman, a doctor of clinical psychology, suggest that very possibility.

Dr. Ekman postulates that facial expressions are governed by a common set of rules and have the same meaning all over the planet. Extensive study in the US, Japan, Brazil, Argentina and the Far East confirmed his theory.

Ekman studied an intricate system of 44 facial muscles that combine to express thousands of nuances of feeling in multiple degrees — joy, sorrow, disgust, smugness, anger, etc.

In collaboration with Wallace V. Friesen, Dr. Ekman devised what he called a *Facial Action Coding System* identifying specific "Action Units" (muscle movements) that produce various facial expressions. In part, their research entailed sitting across from each other and practicing combinations of Action Units to achieve specific expressions. At one point in their studies Ekman and Friesen independently expressed feeling

poorly. It turned out they had been practicing the Action Units for anger and distress. Further research showed that activating the facial muscles associated with anger produced a corresponding elevation of heart rate and increase in heat generating from the palms. Simply arranging the face in an expression of anger produced the symptoms of anger in the body. Physical positioning not only affects experience, but *determines* it!

The body knows a language
the mind never wholly masters.
Brenda Miller

Hold your head up, stand up straight, open your arms wide to the sky and set your face to fun and lightheartedness. What could it hurt?

Once you've mastered the art of evoking a desired feeling, you're ready for action (Step 6). But before we go there I'm going to give you two interim processes (Steps 4 and 5) to ramp up your momentum of success.

It is feeling that imparts vitality to thought.
Charles Haanel

Feelings Menu

abundant	confident	excited
affectionate	content	exhilarated
aligned	courageous	fascinated
amused	creative	fearless
appealing	curious	festive
authentic	daring	flexible
ardent	dashing	free
avid	delicious	frisky
balanced	delighted	fulfilled
blissful	eager	fun
bold	ease	generous
brave	ecstatic	giddy
buoyant	elated	glorious
calm	elegant	grateful
carefree	eloquent	happy
cheerful	empowered	humorous
close	energetic	independent
comfortable	enriched	inquisitive
competent	enthusiastic	inspired
intrigued	peaceful	serene
intuitive	playful	sexy
joyful	pleased	silly
light	productive	sincere
lively	proud	spirited
loving	refreshed	successful
luxurious	rejuvenated	vibrant
mindful	relaxed	vital
nourished	relief	witty
open	restful	wise
optimistic	satisfied	worthy
passionate	secure	zesty

Full Bloom – by Nina Durfee

Recap

- Feeling inspires action.
- *Why* adds incentive and momentum.
- You can change the way you feel by using:
  - Memory
  - Imagination
  - Affirmation
  - Physical posturing

TRY THIS

Add the Why

- Choose an item from your To-Do list that makes you groan when you think about it.

- Close your eyes. Inhale to a count of three, exhale to a count of five. Repeat three to five times.

- Imagine the specific To-Do is already done. (Put yourself "on the beach.")

- What shift do you notice in your body or facial posture?

- What emotion does "doneness" elicit?

- From this better feeling place, what simple initial action are you inspired to take regarding your To-Do? Do it.

- Have FUN guiding your own experience!

STEP 4
Write It Down – Shaping the Shoot

Pretend that you are a writer and that whatever you
write will be performed exactly as you write it.
Esther and Jerry Hicks

When sprouts first appear in a garden, they all look very much alike. It's hard to tell the weeds from the planted seeds. A little time and a little water grow and define the shoots. Once we clearly identify them, we can weed out what we don't want and nurture what we do.

Concrete expression gives substance to thought.

There are a variety of ways to give substance to your vision. What method feels best to you?

Words

Nothing lends credence to an idea quite like seeing it in black and white. As humans we love a good story, whether we are on the receiving end or the telling end. Though we go in knowing that fiction is only make believe, we eagerly turn to Chapter One and suspend disbelief for the sole purpose of being entertained. As you write the vision of your desire, spare no delightful detail. Include color, taste, sound and smell so outrageous as to evoke laughter. Entertain yourself and have fun with it. This is the ultimate game of pretend!

Through writing you define, clarify and refine. When a plant droops, a shot of water brings it erect. Writing is the sprinkle of freshness that fuels expectation.

Something important occurs when we choose to
commit words to paper (or screen);
our inner voice crystallizes into formed ideas.
This alchemical process creates clarity of thought
and allows inner wisdom to come through.
Susan Piver

Written and spoken words are physical manifestations of thought. Words shape ideas like a riverbank gives shape to flowing water. Writing channels attention and directs the path of progress.

Writing enhances awareness. Sometimes I want something at the grocery store, but I don't like to go for just one thing. So I ask my husband what else we need. He rattles off some things and I write them down so I won't forget. Off I go. I return with everything on the list except what I originally intended to buy — because I didn't put it on the list. Conversely, if I make a list but leave it home, I still get everything on the list. Writing it down makes it active in my awareness.

I have a cousin who writes things down because it "takes it out of my mind so that I don't have to think about it." Her daughter, on the other hand, carries it "all in my head" — commendable, but how long can you keep it up? Carrying it all in the head clutters thinking and increases stress, frustration and, to use the word so brilliantly coined in the Hicks books, overwhelment. Writing it down frees the mind and offers instant relief!

In her book *Write it Down, Make it Happen: Knowing What You Want — And Getting It!*, Henriette Anne Klauser advises us to make our list of what we want and attach a why to each item. Why elevates the desire from whiny need to worthy aspiration and sets a fire of inspiration that heightens our senses to opportunity. Clarity of purpose opens awareness of means, opportunity and resources.

Think of what and why as features and benefits. A promotion, greater income and a nicer office are features. Benefits are greater confidence, respect, creative freedom, empowerment and financial ease. Notice how you feel as you write the benefits of what you want. Does your forehead relax? Do you feel relief? You've just succeeded in changing how you feel in the moment!

Interesting tidbit about writing:

Writing with pen and paper engages the right side of the brain (the creative side).
Typing engages the left side (analytical).
Which way feels best to you?

Pictures

Michele Landers, Certified Life Purpose Coach and author of The Tao of Numbers, wanted a house but couldn't afford one. She paged through magazines, cut out a floor plan that she liked and placed it on her refrigerator. "A year or so later," she says, "I was moving into a home. I had all but forgotten about the frayed picture on the refrigerator, which now was behind kids' drawings, calendars, etc. As I removed the papers from the refrigerator . . . this frayed picture of my dream house floor plan floated down to the floor. When I picked it up I was stunned to see it was the exact floor plan of the house I was moving into."

Be there

Want a new car? Enjoy the feeling by test driving one.

Want to move across the country? Visit and explore the city you want to live in.

Want to go to Italy? Take a class in conversational Italian.

Diana Cloud and her husband, of Sarasota, Florida, were ready to own a home on the bay. Money was their obstacle, but "never did we let the idea of insufficient money keep us from dreaming." They found a magnificent bay lot and "one day we dragged lawn chairs onto it. We sat there at sunset with a bottle of wine and talked into the night about what it would be like to build our home there, how much fun it would be to have instant access to the bay, the fun our children would have living on the water and having access to things like fishing, crabs, sea grass and all the other amazing forms of life that abound in and near salt water." Not more than a month later they were making their way to owning that very lot.

Words, pictures and "being there" imprint our awareness and enhance our ability to recognize the bud as a potential blossom. Have fun creating the mini-model of your choice. Read it, see it, touch it, enjoy it. Feel what it will be like when you are there.

> *Vision without action is a daydream;*
> *action without vision is a nightmare.*
> Japanese Proverb

Recap

- Concrete expression gives substance to thought.
- Writing enhances awareness.
- Writing frees the mind.
- Words, pictures and "being there" imprint our awareness and enhance our ability to recognize the bud as a potential blossom.

TRY THIS

Create a Vision Board

- Tools you will need:
  - Poster board
  - Magazines
  - Scissors
  - Glue

- Cut out photos, words, shapes and colors that feel good to you relative to what you want to change.

- Paste them onto the poster board in a layout that is pleasing to you.

- Display the collage where you can see it daily.

- Notice and enjoy how you feel when you look at it.

- Appreciate your freedom to express!

STEP 5
Allow – Let Nature Take its Course

Let it be.
John Lennon

You're off to a good start. The first stages of creation are at play. You have put it in black and white, and you have imagined and experienced the sensations that will prevail. Now watch as opportunities, options, meetings, information and people assemble to accommodate your desire.

Let go and trust the process.

> *All you have to do is decide what it is you would like*
> *to experience, and then allow it in order to achieve it.*
> Esther and Jerry Hicks

Once you plant a sunflower seed, you don't dig up the root to see if it's strong. You don't tug on it to make it taller. You don't pry open the bud. You allow nature to take its course. You trust the process.

Allowing means letting go of self-imposed resistance. Long-time habits of resistant thought have created an Emotional Setpoint of doubt that blocks the achievement of what you want. It is easier to trust your creative process if your Emotional Setpoint is something other than doubt or worry.[2]

Your Emotional Setpoint determines your experience.

Your Emotional Setpoint is your dominant emotion, what you most regularly feel or practice either in general or with respect to a particular subject. In *Ask and It Is Given: Learning to Manifest Your Desires*, Hicks suggests a range of emotions that can help you determine this primary

---

[2] According to medical research conducted in 2007 by pain expert Dr. Greg Fors, the term "setpoint" is useful both physiologically and psychologically. This makes sense if we believe in the mind-body connection. Examples are body weight and happiness — two elements that medical experts believe have setpoints that are difficult to change.

emotion. At the high end of the scale are joy, knowledge, empowerment, freedom, love and appreciation. The scale descends from there through enthusiasm/eagerness, positive expectation, optimism, contentment, boredom, pessimism, frustration/irritation/impatience, overwhelment, worry, blame, anger, revenge, hatred/rage, jealousy, insecurity/guilt/unworthiness, and fear, depression or powerlessness.

The Law of Attraction automatically draws to you the essence of your Emotional Setpoint.

> *Worry has been accurately described as*
> *praying for what you don't want*
> *and is perhaps the ultimate negative affirmation.*
> Guy Spiro
> *www.lightworks.com*

If your Emotional Setpoint is worry, the Law of Attraction will bring more for you to worry about. The bright side is, regardless of your Emotional Setpoint, you have the power to change it. It just takes practice.

To change your Emotional Setpoint, shift focus from what to why.

When I read *The Secret* by Rhonda Byrne, I desperately wanted to believe that I could simply envision money and it would come to me. I tested the theory by imagining $25,000 landing in my hands. I crafted affirmations. I closed my eyes and saw my bank statement registering the deposit. I printed a "check" dated December 25 and wrote "Merry Christmas with love" on the memo line of the check. Christmas came and went. No $25,000.

In retrospect, I realize the "Merry Christmas with love" was my version of tugging on the plant to make it taller. I didn't trust that things could change unless I could identify a logical pathway. Clearly, I didn't let go and allow. Instead, I held a vision that limited my options.

After Christmas I reevaluated. I released the how and literally opened my arms to welcome abundance from wherever it might come. I printed another check as if it were drawn on my own bank account. I put it under a magnet on the refrigerator and did my best to forget about it.

Within a month we accepted an offer to buy our lathe and mill that had sat unused for three years. Simultaneously we received an insurance check in settlement of our son's fender bender. Suddenly our bank account held over $10,000. It wasn't $25,000, but it was five figures in an account that had been accustomed to three, often in red.

I felt exhilarating freedom and relief. I had my husband look at our bank balance. "Woo hoo!" he yodeled. And then he delivered the punch. "But the money's going to be gone tomorrow, right?"

We both knew that credit cards and medical bills would eat up the money. "But let's savor the moment," I pleaded. We committed that balance to memory and vowed to get used to it — the more commas, the better!

The next day the money was gone (as were a good portion of the bills) and life went on. We basked in the euphoria of debt reduction and financial relaxation, remembering the vision and enjoying the feeling. Less than a month later our bank balance again hit five figures. We paid down more credit and student loans and really began to taste abundance.

What I learned was to change the weight of my request from what and how to why. I reached beyond reasons like getting out of debt, affording a bigger house, and fear of living out retirement as a street person. I recognized my real desire — worry-free bill paying (financial ease), cavorting with cousins on the opposite coast (family connection), and choice (freedom) to spend my time as I want without mandate from someone else. I learned to let go of self-imposed habits of resistance and my requirement to know and understand the specific logic of manifestation. I allowed for possibility.

Once I shifted my default focus an interesting thing transpired. A cousin's wedding brought a gaggle of East Coast relatives literally to my West Coast backyard. I enjoyed the benefit (frolic with the family) without the worry of amassing the money or the time to travel. I felt freedom and relief in the manifestation of joyful experience in spite of financial "truth."

With enough attention to anything,
the essence of what you have been giving thought to
will eventually become a physical manifestation.
Esther and Jerry Hicks

A story of powerful allowing

I cannot over-emphasize the importance of allowing in the creative process. *But what if my spouse wants something different than I want? Will neither of us get what we want?* I thought you'd never ask!

Remember the long list of desires I mentioned in the Forward to this book? One that felt particularly baffling to me was moving to the Puget Sound area from the open valley farm country where we lived. I wanted to move for a number of reasons, one being that my cousin, like a sister to me, and three of my very close girlfriends lived in the Seattle area. I ached to spend more time with all of them.

The challenge was that my husband loved where we lived and especially enjoyed playing guitar and singing with dear friends nearby. He had no inclination to move. I wrestled with the disparity between my dream and his and with the seeming contradiction of my wanting to move and my desire not to lose touch with our close musical friends. I could not figure out how to reconcile the opposing desires. Much like my experience in the downward spiraling airplane, I could do nothing but throw up my hands in surrender.

I re-framed my intention. I shifted focus from specific features (the kind of house, the location, the people, the clientele, the money, etc.) to the essence or the why of what I wanted — the benefits. I focused on the energizing freshness of big-bodied water, mountains and lush greenery. I focused on laughing and engaging with people who "get" me. I focused on the spiritual stimulation of cultural and intellectual diversity.

I brought my husband into my vision. I focused on the growth and deepening of our love and relationship. I focused on easy, joyful engagement in work and play for each of us and for both of us. I imagined us engaging in soul-feeding activity. I imagined feeling ease around our finances, our relationships and our life work.

Full Bloom – by Nina Durfee

I nurtured this all-inclusive vision briefly — maybe a matter of weeks — and then the most amazing thing happened. I came home from work one day to find my husband surfing Craigslist for jobs in the Seattle area. Within a month he was offered a position that thrilled him and he couldn't wait to make the move!

My husband now loves his work in an independent-living and aging-care facility, where he plays and sings for the residents and staff. He enjoys our proximity to open water and fishing, and he enjoys regular connection with buddies who share his interests. I love my work life and my life work and my regular connection with my cousin and friends.

My husband and I periodically visit or are visited by our good musical friends from the old neighborhood. We feel greater ease in our finances and living environment. Our relationship grows deeper and richer, our communication is more clear, and our dreams are growing and unfolding in ways that feel better and better.

I do not pretend to know or understand the multiplicity of forces that overlapped to assemble what seemed to me impossible. What I do know is that I feel a direct relationship between my ability to allow and what comes true for me.

Observe.

Once you have expressed desire, the Law of Attraction assembles the elements that light up pathways and create opportunities for you. Whether you notice them or not depends on your Emotional Setpoint. If you stay in a place of doubt, worry and self-pity, you can't see opportunity. When you release self-imposed resistance, say through meditation, your murky vision becomes clear and options become apparent.

Consider fingerprints. You leave them on everything you touch: table tops, silverware, book jackets, remote control, hair brush, coffee cup, keyboard, steering wheel. Mostly you don't see them. But if you apply the magic dust and special light they pop into view. Intentional observation *invites* the appearance of the prints.

If you are like most people, you think that to produce a result you have to do something specific: make phone calls, schedule events, organize papers, convince others, follow protocols, ask for money, save money, pay money. In a nutshell you believe you have to control circumstances. But when you busy yourself from a sense of duty ("I should" or "I have to") in order to control outcome, you are at odds with yourself, and you restrict the flow of easy accomplishment.

Don't beat yourself up. You are not alone. Someone important to you set that example, and you've practiced it well. Good girl. Now drop that belief like somebody else's dirty laundry. It no longer serves you! Your new practice is to trust the power of your intention and the certainty of the Law of Attraction. Blind trust is neither easy nor necessary. Simply observe from a place of curiosity and watch what happens.

Recognize.

Once you have expressed a clear desire and made it visually concrete by writing or journaling or creating a collage, set an intention to recognize options as opposed to manipulating circumstances. In the case of writing and publishing this book, I noticed the inspired idea for a chapter; I had a moment of clarity in which the jacket blurb nearly wrote itself; *Publishers' Weekly* announced an upsurge in self-discovery books; writers' conferences came to my home town; I connected with people who knew exactly what I wanted to learn.

All of those resources were available before I ever thought about writing this book. My intention plus attention were the magic dust and special light that opened my eyes to options.

The bud looks nothing like the flower, but its presence promises full bloom. My desire for more money and the ability to travel to visit family manifested as cousins coming to me without my spending a dime. I got the *benefit* of what I wanted. I could whine that I still couldn't afford to travel, but that would shift my focus away from the joy of having what I wanted in the first place. If we don't recognize the bud, we risk missing the joy of full bloom.

The elements of your dream are here now, waiting for you to connect. Be aware. *Allow* by letting go of self-imposed resistance. *Observe* with an intention to see. Be curious. *Recognize* and delight in the options!

Through allowing. . .you become whole.
Eckhart Tolle

- Let go and allow.
- Trust the process.
- Your Emotional Setpoint determines your experience.
- To change your Emotional Setpoint, shift focus from *what* to *why*.
- Observe from a place of curiosity.
- Recognize and delight in the options.

TRYTHIS

Change Your Emotional Setpoint

- Wrap your arms around yourself and curl into a fetal position. Squeeze tightly as if to keep your inner worries from escaping. What happens to your breath? Your circulation? Your facial expression?

- Stand up straight, open your arms wide and extend your fingers as far as you can reach, as if to let the worry go. What happens to your breath? Your circulation? Your facial expression?

- From this open position, make an affirmative statement that feels good. For example: "I release worry. I invite ease."

- With arms still wide open, breathe in deeply and exhale long.

- Enjoy your day — allowing, observing and recognizing.

STEP 6
Act – Fertilization

*How we spend our days is, of course,
how we spend our lives.*
Annie Dillard

Enjoyment in the process ensures enjoyment in the outcome.

Options and opportunities abound. They lie before you like a bowl of jellybeans, a delightful abundance of assorted colors and flavors to choose from. How do you choose? I go for the black jellybeans first because licorice is my favorite. When books jump at you from the shelves and experts cross your path and creative ideas surface in the wee morning hours, act on the option that feels best — not because of its potential outcome, but because *doing it* feels good. Enjoyment in the process ensures enjoyment in the outcome.

*The only reason for time is so that
everything doesn't happen at once.*
Albert Einstein

Face it — you can't do everything at once. In fact you can't do everything, period. And who wants to, anyway? Consider your level of enthusiasm for each option. What feels fun? What are you eager to dive into? The outcome from action born of enthusiasm is exponentially more satisfying than the outcome from action born of guilt, duty or what someone else thinks you should be doing. Choose fun and save drudgery for later. Progress is as much what we leave behind as what we take on.

When I began testing the process of intentional manifestation with respect to my life work, I dutifully responded to every opportunity. I ran frantically from meeting to meeting, chased down leads, committed to workshops, wrote articles, joined writing groups, booked speaking engagements. Result: acute overwhelment.

Just say no.

In an effort to keep too many plates spinning, I felt discouraged, depleted and desperate. I threw up my hands and cried help! What crossed my path was a book by William Ury called *The Power of a Positive No: Save the Deal, Save the Relationship — and Still Say No.* Although I never found time to read it before it was due back at the library, the title's simple suggestion that it might be okay to say no empowered me to decide how I felt about my pending commitments. My feelings ranged from "can't wait to dive in" to "don't make me do it!" I narrowed my list to a few favorites and permitted myself to let the others go.

Fascinating, what happened next. Projects that I decided to unhook from dissolved all by themselves. The writers' group that was draining my energy nearly disbanded before my eyes. The business group for which I was reluctantly considering serving as an officer changed policies and format, and I never had to make the decision. And the multiple daily email offers that I had previously found addicting lost their appeal. I triumphantly and repeatedly clicked "unsubscribe." I found relief as white space appeared in my calendar, and I had more clarity around steps that I felt would be fun. Granting yourself permission to let go opens a channel of ease and flow.

> *Just say no.*
> Nancy Reagan

At first it wasn't easy to unplug from old habits. I engaged with a coach who helped me clarify intention, design a balanced action plan and stay on track. My coach held me accountable, assessed progress and helped me adjust course as needed. My coach helped me replace old debilitating beliefs with new empowering affirmations and habits. The impact of the coaching process on me was so powerful it inspired me to become a coach myself. Now I joyfully facilitate that same process for others.

Act not from motivation but from inspiration.

Motivation compels us to act for the sake of something outside us — to attain a physical result or to please someone else. Motivation feels like "should." No matter how tempting the end result seems, if the action feels like drudgery, the outcome will fail to satisfy.

Full Bloom – by Nina Durfee

Inspiration stems from passion. Inspiration compels us from the inside to act *for the joy of acting.* Inspiration feels like "yippee!" Inspired action is exhilarating and satisfying in both the doing and in the end result.

Apply the "feel good" test.

The Law of Attraction brings you more of whatever you focus on. Do what feels like drudgery, and you attract boredom and dissatisfaction. Do what feels stimulating and exciting, and more stimulation and excitement come your way.

Skeptical? Conduct your own experiment. Apply the "feel good" test over and over and notice what happens with your dominant emotion and the flow of productivity and accomplishment. When we feel better, even tasks that previously seemed monumental or distasteful become less of a big deal and are easier to complete.

A wise person said, "You always have energy for the next right step." Inspired action energizes like the fertilizer that brightens foliage, opens the bud and sweetens the fruit.

> *Just work on whatever you want most right now.*
> Martha Beck

Recap

- Enjoyment in the process ensures enjoyment in the outcome.
- Progress is as much what we leave behind as what we take on.
- Just say no.
- Granting yourself permission allows ease and flow.
- Motivation feels like "should." Inspiration feels like "yippee!"
- Apply the "feel good" test.

TRY THIS

Let Go and Allow

- Tools you will need:
  - Pen or pencil
  - Sheet of paper
  - Scissors or paper shredder or blazing fireplace

- Think of an area of your life that feels dissatisfying (for example, job).

- Draw a line down the middle of the paper to create two columns. In the left column list reasons for your dissatisfaction (for example, work is boring, my co-worker is rude, my boss doesn't trust me, I'm underpaid).

- For each description in the left column, use the right column to describe what you want instead. For example, intellectual stimulation, harmonious relationships, confidence, worthiness or abundance. Use the *Feelings Menu* at the end of Step 3 to help clarify your expression.

- For each pair of opposites, say aloud a complete statement to the effect of "I'm willing to let go of [boredom] so that I can allow and enjoy [intellectual stimulation]."

- Cut the page in half along the center dividing line. Shred the strip of negative words or throw it into the blazing fireplace. Feel the physical and emotional space that opens as you let them go.

- Look again at the list of positive emotions. Feel them expand into the open space created by the release of negative feelings. Decide how you will carry these positive feelings with you wherever you go.

STEP 7

Enjoy! — The Glory of Full Bloom

Life is here to enjoy!
Maharishi Mahesh Yogi

There's no getting around it: action produces results. Action taken by default offers random results. Inspired, intentional action reaps satisfaction.

Assess progress.

If you've given the first six steps a whirl, your awareness and experience are different from when you started. What has changed? Whether your intended desire manifested spot on or fell a little short, the result is your creation. Acknowledge your part in the process. Assess the success of your endeavors by asking these questions:

Step 1 – Be still. *Do I enjoy stillness/meditation on a regular basis?* Regularity and enjoyment produce faster results.

Step 2 – Think. *What mental tapes do I play?* When you catch yourself in negative mind chatter, replace it with thoughts that feel better.

Step 3 – Feel. *When I decide what I want, am I articulating why?* Put yourself "on the beach" and enjoy the feeling.

Step 4 – Write it down. *Am I making my dream concrete?* Escape fully into your game of pretend by using words, pictures or actions.

Step 5 – Allow. *Am I getting out of my own way?* Worry is self-imposed resistance. Shift your Emotional Setpoint from worry to ease.

Step 6 – Act. *Am I acting by default or by design?* Act not from motivation, but from inspiration.

Don't take yourself too seriously.

It is tempting to dwell on what appear to be failures, but frankly they are just not that important. What is important is to learn from them and let them go. Focus on what works. Be curious and excited to craft your next experience.

> *Life is too important to be taken seriously.*
> Oscar Wilde

When I envisioned moving to the Puget Sound area, I included in my written description "big water views." What I didn't include was "from my living room window." We don't have water views from our home, but I see Lake Washington from my high-rise office. I enjoy what I have now — and I'll be more specific next time. The important thing is to have fun in the game.

Take credit.

Acknowledge your part in creating your experience. Bask in the knowledge that you do, in fact, mold your own reality. How empowering is that!

In the event your end result is less than you hoped for, take credit for that too. Then look for ways to fine tune the process. Acknowledge your Emotional Setpoint as your point of attraction and recognize your power to elevate it. Open your arms, receive what comes, and watch with curiosity how life expands before your eyes into something even better than you dreamed.

Bask!

A single sunflower seed may produce a single flower or a stemful of blossoms. Receive the gift. Enjoy the beauty.

> *Acknowledging the good that is already in your life*
> *is the foundation for all abundance.*
> Eckhart Tolle

Revel in the difference between the empowerment of deliberate creation versus the old wing-and-a-prayer take-what-comes method. Enjoy molding the clay. What are you eager to create next? Welcome to life by design!

Joy is the best makeup.
Anne Lamott

Recap

- Assess progress.
- Don't take yourself too seriously.
- Have fun in the game.
- Take credit.
- Bask!

TRY THIS

Acknowledge Your Power

- Pay attention to little "outcomes" during your day. How did the meeting go? What did the meal taste like? What did she say about my performance?

- When an outcome is less than satisfying, acknowledge: I did that.

- When an outcome is satisfying, acknowledge: I did that.

- Delight in your power to mold your experience.

+1 TO GROW ON
Appreciate – Perpetuating Abundance

All you need is love.
The Beatles

Your sunflower patch yields a harvest of beautiful bouquets and plentiful seeds. You collect the seeds, dry them, roast and salt them, savor the flavor and share the yummies with family and friends. There are plenty left over to plant another crop. Seeds are nature's built-in promise for more. Seeds perpetuate abundance.

Appreciation perpetuates fulfillment.

Appreciation is joy unabridged. Perpetuate it by expressing it. Appreciate the learning, the experience and the powerful feeling of sculpting your own reality. Liberally sprinkle appreciative thoughts and comments on all the contributing players: colleagues, friends, angels, God, the Universe.

A state of appreciation is pure connection to Source
where there is no perception of lack.
Esther and Jerry Hicks

Appreciation feels good.

How does appreciation work? When I say thank you out of habit, I get a programmed you're welcome. When I say it with sincerity, it settles more deeply. When I feel appreciation inside, my chest expands. Appreciation feeds the soul. Appreciation feels good.

You get what you practice.

The Law of Attraction brings us what we continue to focus on. Appreciation expressed attracts more to appreciate. Give joy, receive joy, repeat. What a great system!

Heartfelt thanks elevates the vibrations of both the giver and the receiver. It opens a channel of love and abundance for both. Appreciation carves a

connecting loop — not just a circle, but an expanding upward spiral of abundance that fulfills both giver and receiver.

What do you appreciate? Is it something as simple as socks or something as profound and intimate as feet on which to wear them? Little leads to big. Make a list of what you appreciate. Feel the goodness of it. The more you notice, the greater your fulfillment.

Appreciation enhances the creative process.

Appreciation enhances the power of each of the seven practical steps to get what you want. Don't save it for the end. Sprinkle it liberally throughout the process to enhance your enjoyment on the journey. Appreciate the restfulness of meditation; appreciate the clarity of inspired thought; appreciate the power of memory, imagination, affirmation and physical posturing to shift how you feel; have fun writing your story, collecting photos, and hanging around in the neighborhood of what you want; stand in awe when options assemble before your eyes; feel the fun of inspired action and the relief of letting go of drudgery; relax in the ease and flow of eager curiosity; bask in the outcome, no matter how similar or different from your original intention.

When you live from an attitude of appreciation, you readily open wide to explore, embrace and realize deeper joy and exuberance. Attune to appreciation, and your postures of defensiveness and resistance melt away like sore muscles loosening up in a warm bath. In that state of allowing, you feel the rich abundant flow of wisdom, health, love, satisfaction, passion and joy. When you let go, allow and appreciate, the cells of your body and the petals of your mind and heart open to receive the ever-present blessings of a life in **Full Bloom**.

There will come a time
when you believe everything is finished.
That will be the beginning.
Louis L'Amour

Recap

- Appreciation perpetuates fulfillment.
- Appreciation feels good.
- You get what you practice.
- Appreciation enhances the process.

TRY THIS

Perpetuate Abundance

- Be aware when you are in "pause" mode – holding on a phone call, waiting in line, between activities, doing a mundane task like chopping vegetables, brushing your teeth or driving a distance.

- Breathe deeply in and out, and have a contest with yourself to recognize how many things you appreciate in the moment.

- Notice how awareness of one appreciated thing draws ideas of more to appreciate. For example, some things to appreciate about chopping vegetables:

  - Efficiency of a sharp knife
  - Pleasing assortment of colors and aromas
  - Eager anticipation of taste
  - Convenience of assorted vegetables at one store
  - Co-creation that makes it possible: farmers, harvesters, oil companies that fuel the machinery, delivery truck drivers, building contractors, shelf stockers, checkout clerks
  - Planet Earth with fertile soil, water and nourishment
  - Unseen forces that deliver sunshine and rain and keep the Earth spinning in its orbit

- Enjoy the perpetuation of abundance through appreciation!

Afterword

Although these steps are presented in what appears to be logical order, the fact is that each step stands alone as a powerful tool to move you forward from wherever you are.

Don't get caught up in the details of the process. Be easy with it. Notice. Pay attention. Appreciate. Apply these seven-plus-one steps to create everything you want physically, mentally, emotionally and spiritually. Enjoy the full blossom of life!

Live not by default, but by design!

About the Author

Nina Durfee is a personal development coach certified through the International Coach Federation. Seeking and applying wisdom that pertains directly to what she wants, Nina celebrates life-long learning.

As the founder of LifeSculpt (www.LifeSculpt. net) and co-founder of The Wisdom Well Retreats, LLC (www.WisdomWellRetreats.com), Nina works internationally and virtually to empower women to turn passion into productivity, to do what they love and love what they do, and to live not by default, but by design.

Nina believes it is important to laugh, especially at ourselves. "Life is a work in progress," she says, "and if it ever reaches completion there will be no place else to go, so we'd better darn well enjoy the ride!"

Nina's Guiding Principle: *Don't take yourself too seriously*!

Nina's secret to success: *Appreciation*.

To schedule a free strategy session or enroll in a coaching program or Full Bloom Playshop, go to www.LifeSculpt.net.

[inside back cover - blank]

"[Full Bloom] built beautiful images in my mind, took me back to my childhood. The steps make great sense!"

Kristie Morgan, Seattle, WA

"Full Bloom is concise, clear, spot on and beautiful. I appreciate the silence between the words."

Beth Taylor, Global Resource Group.

"Divinely inspired. Awesome. Lovely, gorgeous. Simple, soul-full."

Fran Fisher, Master Certified Coach, Bellevue, WA, author of Violet's Vision

Have you ever wanted something so badly you could taste it? Do you ever feel frustrated that you can't find the perfect mate, that you don't communicate effectively with your children, that prosperity eludes you, that your business or career falls short of your ideal?

Have you ever wished it were easier to get what you want?

Driven by the desire to create powerful positive change in her own life, Nina Durfee has read the self-help books, listened to the inspirational speakers, tested the practices and mined countless gems of wisdom. Based on her own experience of what works and what doesn't work, Nina has solidified abstract wisdom into concrete action steps and offers an easy, effective and practical pathway from desire to fulfillment.

Whether you want an ideal relationship, career satisfaction, financial ease or a new way of being, this simple process is tried and true. Employ these *7 Practical Steps +1 to Grow On* and watch in delight as the life you desire blossoms before your eyes.